Agenda 2030 Uncovered (2021-2050)

Economic Crisis, Hyperinflation, Fuel and Food Shortage, World Wars and Cyber Attacks

(The Great Reset & Techno-Fascist Future Explained)

Rebel Press Media

Disclaimer

Our other books

Check out our other books for other unreported news, exposed facts and debunked truths, and more.

Join the exclusive Rebel Press Media Circle!

You will get a new updates about the unreported reality delivered in your inbox every Friday.

Sign up here today:

https://campsite.bio/rebelpressmedia

Introduction

'Unless something drastic changes, the world will undoubtedly witness the first nuclear conflict in the 2020s.'

The "Great Reset" has been planned to extend current decaying system, but it will fail" - U.S., German, and British populations substantially wiped out by 2025, riches gone - "West seeks to instigate conflict with Russia to retain own hegemony, but it will fail"

Years ago, we were first drawn to the pessimistic predictions of Deagel.com, a private geopolitical and military intelligence site that relies on official figures, reports, and documents from the CIA, the US Department of Defense, the World Bank, the World Economic Forum, the EU, the IMF, and just about every other credible international body and organization, among others. Nothing appears to have changed since the September 2020 update: the West is still in total collapse in 2025, while the intensity of the blow varies from country to country.

The United States, the United Kingdom, and Germany will be particularly hard hit, while the Netherlands and Finland will be spared. Nonetheless, Deagel estimates that approximately 1 million people will perish in our country.

Deagel predicted in 2014 that the Western bloc on both sides of the Atlantic would collapse by 2025 as a result of unrestricted money printing and debt. That fate remains unavoidable. Furthermore, the Corona crisis has demonstrated that "the Western world's success model is predicated on civilizations lacking resilience, which can barely bear any adversity, even of little intensity." This is something we assumed, and now we have unequivocal evidence.'

The Great Reset is a method of temporarily extending the life of a dying system.

'Through the so-called Great Reset, which, like climate change, extinction uprising, planetary crisis, 'green revolution,' and shale oil hoaxes, is propagated by the establishment, the Covid crisis will be utilized to extend the life of this failing economic system.'

If you want to know more about the exact goals and predicted future of the great reset, please check out our other books on the subject, you can find them under our publisher's name "Rebel Press Media" at all major book retailers.

Everything about the 'Great Reset,' including the corona lockdowns and the purposeful annihilation of the hospitality, tourism, and most of the SME sector, is intended at rapidly reversing the spending economy so that we may continue on more or less the same footing for a few more years. 'That might work for a while, but it won't cure the basic issue and will merely postpone the inevitable.' The ruling elite only wants to stay in power, which is all that matters to them.'

'Covid has demonstrated that the West is incapable of dealing with adversity.'

'Through a convergence of problems, the collapse of the Western banking system - and ultimately Western civilization - is the fundamental element in the prophecy, and it has a disastrous end.' Covid has demonstrated that diversity and radical liberalism have rendered Western civilizations incapable of dealing with actual adversity.'

Deagel uses the Spanish flu pandemic of nearly a century ago as an illustration. It killed between 40 and 50 million people. Now since the world's population is four times higher, corona would have killed at least 160 million to 200 million people if it had been just as terrible (given globalism and intensive air travel, twice that is more likely). However, the (possibly artificially exaggerated) death toll now stands at 2.9 million, or 0.037 percent of the world's population, which is equal to a weak seasonal flu outbreak.

'Most wealthy nations will pay largest price'

'It's extremely likely that the global economic catastrophe caused by the lockdowns would kill more people than the virus,' Deagel claims. 'The harsh reality of the diverse and varied Western society is that a collapse will take a toll of 50 percent to 80 percent, depending on numerous conditions' (of the population). Overall, the most diverse, multicultural, indebted welfare states (with the highest standards of living) will pay the heaviest price.'

Only 'over-consumption,' with huge doses of boundless degeneracy packaged as virtue, keeps our strange, erroneous Western culture together like 'glue.' 'Hate legislation' and contradicting signals suggest that, despite considerable censoring, this glue is no longer effective. However, not everyone has to die; migration can also be beneficial.'

Analysts predict that countries in the Second and Third Worlds that stick to the "Old World Order" will fall in line with the West. However, because these countries are poorer, the impact will be much milder. Furthermore, these are frequently still homogeneous (cohesive) civilizations, which have historically been significantly more resilient to large systemic crises or other disasters. Countries that look to China have the best chance of quickly regaining stability.

World War 3 is the 'most likely event in the 2020s,' according to experts.

Russia and China have begun to develop a strategic economic and military alliance, despite the EU opposing any reconciliation with Russia for years and even portraying it as an enemy (which will replace the West and form the true New World Order). Contrary to popular belief in the West, Russia and China are already far ahead of the United States and Europe (NATO) in terms of military technology in several sectors.

A new major (world) war is even called "the most likely major event" in these 20s. The first scenario is a conventional war (as is about to break out in Ukraine) escalating to a nuclear war. The second scenario is placed between 2025 and 2030, and assumes an overwhelming Russian surprise attack on the West. To the dismay of the Western military elite, the Russians showed in Syria in 2015 that they are capable of carrying out such an attack to perfection at a distance of more than 2,000 kilometers.

'The irony is that since the end of the Cold War, the US has put NATO in position to carry out such a 'first strike' on Russia, and it now looks like that first strike is indeed going to happen, but the country that will be finished off is the US.'

'Westerners are snobbish and misled.'

'Another feature of the Western society is that its subjects have been brainwashed to the point where the majority has come to accept their moral superiority and technological edge as a given.' This has cleared the way for emotional arguments to triumph over intellectual arguments, which are ignored or dismissed. This thinking could play a big part in the impending disasters.'

'Unless something drastic changes, the world will experience the first nuclear war.'

'Starting a war appears to be a quick and easy way to reclaim lost hegemony. France had not have nuclear weapons in 1940, thus it could not turn a defeat into a victory. Because of the uncomfortable potential of becoming "the dictator and his filthy whore" who fled in terror while the rest of the world laughs at them, the West may try this now.

'Unless something drastic changes, the world will undoubtedly witness the first nuclear war.' The Western bloc's demise could occur before, during, or after the war. It makes no difference. A nuclear war is a risk with billions of victims, and the figure will be in the hundreds of millions during the collapse.'

Table of Contents

Chapter 1: Only 5 years left?

Major (false flag) terror attacks, financial mega-crises, the emergence of the police state, and even a big viral epidemic were all predicted by authors 23 years ago, culminating in a new World War - Why is it that humankind refuses to learn from the past?

Authors William Strauss and Neil Howe demonstrated, using 500 years of Western history, that the rise and collapse of a civilisation follows certain processes and patterns that cannot be avoided time and time again in their 1997 book The Fourth Turning. They anticipated that these historical principles would lead to the demise of Western civilization by 2025.

Up to and including a huge virus breakout, the phases and situations they detailed 23 years ago turned out to be almost chillingly accurate. Is it possible that the last five years of our civilization have arrived?

Unfortunately, all indications are that indeed the last 5 years have arrived.

A well-known proverb goes, "History repeats itself." Strauss and Howe investigated how ancient and modern civilizations thrived, ruled, and eventually vanished. They discovered several striking parallels, such as an 80-year cycle with four distinct phases:

1. The period of prosperity that follows a catastrophic crisis. That was World War II in our instance. As a society, we began to rebuild together. Everyone shared the same ambition: to make a better future for their (grand)children and for themselves. Morale was good, and trust in the government was high. It resulted in a massive increase in the ordinary man's prosperity and well-being.

2. Being aware. This period began in the 1960s, when a rising number of people began to challenge the existing order's norms and ideals, as well as its judgments. We had the "psychedelic" revolution, as well as anti-war demonstrations against wars that were both deadly and futile, such as Vietnam. Protests and civil rights movements gained in popularity.

3. Decomposition. The West emerged from the great crisis of the late 1970s and early 1980s thanks to President Ronald Reagan's economic, financial, and foreign policies, and entered an era of extraordinary growth in the 1990s. In contrast to its heyday, this expansion now mostly benefits "big money," Wall Street, banks, multinational corporations, the powerful elite, and only a few citizens who had to make do with crumbs from the wealth boom.

At the same time, society shifted its emphasis from the communal to the individual, resulting in the self-centered "selfie" and Facebook generations of today, whose lives revolve primarily around their own perceptions, experiences, feelings, contacts, and opinions. The loss of a shared objective, exacerbated in part by the aim of erasing national, social, cultural, and personal borders, resulted in widespread fragmentation in society and politics, as well as an all-encompassing loss of sense of identity.

At the same time, society shifted its emphasis from the communal to the individual, resulting in the self-centered "selfie" and Facebook generations of today, whose lives revolve primarily around their own perceptions, experiences, feelings, contacts, and opinions. The loss of a shared objective, exacerbated in part by the aim of erasing national, social, cultural, and personal borders, resulted in widespread fragmentation in society and politics, as well as an all-encompassing loss of sense of identity. This emptiness proved a breeding ground for the rise of the modern, sectarian religion of "climate change" and other extremist groups such as Black Lives Matter.

4. The start of a crisis. With the onset of the financial crisis in 2008, the final phase began. The politicians used unimaginable amounts of taxpayer money to bail out their bank friends, and most crucially, themselves and their own political beliefs, leaving the people to foot the cost. Several decisions were made against the desire of the majority, including the greater integration of EU member states into a Superstate, the formation of a perpetual flow of money from North to South (Transfer Union), and the large importation of millions of migrants from the Muslim world, and the gradual dismantling of our stable and cheap food and energy supply and prosperity because of a climate problem that has been sucked out of our heads.

From financial crises to terrorist strikes and viral breakouts, almost everything came true.

Take a look at the five major developments and events predicted by Strauss and Howe for phases 3 and 4, which they believe will lead to our civilization's demise:

1. Financial and economic meltdowns. The state raises taxes, seizes residents' assets, and establishes a totalitarian control society. Citizens resist in the final phase (e.g., the Yellow Speakers in France), prompting governments to deploy security forces. The state of siege or some other sort of perpetual state of emergency is eventually imposed.

2. A major terrorist attack on an airline (four years before 9/11) to which the United States reacts with military force. Police and security forces are gaining more and more power, and they are now permitted to regulate and arrest civilians on the streets and subsequently in their homes for no apparent reason. More assaults raise false-flag concerns, prompting charges against the government.

3. Stock market crash. Starting on Wall Street, banks around the world collapse, and governments are forced to take on massive debts at the expense of society in order to "rescue" these institutions. (In 2008, this came to pass.) The second financial crisis began in the EU in 2015, when the ECB implemented negative interest rates. The next 'hot' financial crisis, which will be utilized to fully digitize money movement, is expected to occur in 2021).

4. Virus outbreak. A new dangerous sickness is fast spreading, and it will be used to justify large-scale quarantines (lockdowns) and other authoritarian policies, robbing residents of nearly all their liberties.

5. Armed conflict. Russia reclaims control of the anarchic former Soviet republics (which did not happen) and creates a strategic partnership with Iran (also did not happen). Military clashes all over the world (which have occurred: Iraq, Afghanistan, Syria, Yemen, Libya, Azerbaijan-Armenia, China-US military tensions, China-Japan, China-India, India-Pakistan, US/NATO-Russia, US/Israel/Saudi Arabia-Iran, Turkey-India) result in brutal wars, which could lead to World War III.

The Fourth Turning Point has begun.

As a result, the "Fourth Turning Point" in the United States and Europe is well underway, and appears to have reached its conclusion (2020-2025). For years, society has been becoming more insecure and violent. People become increasingly polarized into increasingly radical 'right' and 'left' camps, with the 'right' wanting to return to a more stable, prosperous period when they still had a say in the future of their own countries, and the 'left' wanting to demolish all existing structures, with mass immigration, climate policy, and 'diversity' as their main weapons.

The 'politically correct' opinion terror of the government and mainstream media, which certainly in 2020 will function purely as a 'Ministry of Propaganda', ensures in the meantime that an ever-growing group of people, who are concerned about the developments and decisions that are made over and over again, are put in a corner and ignored and/or blackened as 'extreme right-wing racists' or 'conspiracy theorists'.

After all, leftist politics aspires to gain power by violence.

Following Donald Trump's stunning election victory over Hillary Clinton, the candidate of the "Deep State" shadow government, well-organized mass protests (Antifa, Black Lives Matter) erupted, financed by extreme left globalist George Soros, in the hopes of preventing Trump's re-election by causing as much chaos and violence as possible.

Patriotic "right-wing" America is still largely silent, but analysts believe that a sizable number of Trump supporters are prepared to defend their president, particularly if the Democrats, with the help of the media they control, stage a coup by declaring Joe Biden the winner after November 3, even if Trump had won a massive victory. Violent clashes are unavoidable, and some analysts are even predicting a new civil war and the probable division of the United States into many sections. This will have far-reaching implications for Europe as well.

It is morals, not technology, that defines civilization.

Many people make the mistake of focusing solely on technological advancements ("Look at all that new smart technology!") and superficial socioeconomic conditions ("We're still doing pretty well, aren't we?") when assessing a civilization's health. However, these are not the most important indicators of a civilization's health. This is because the mentality and morality of both the people and their leaders constantly stands or falls - literally.

Politicians who are no longer ashamed of self-enrichment, lies, and deceptions (much alone resigning), but who employ them as a matter of course, are usually at the forefront of the decline. Election promises and platforms that are either completely unfulfilled or reversed. Without consulting the public, treaties and choices that harm society and sovereignty are pushed through. Freedoms are being progressively reduced, or perhaps taken away entirely, on various pretexts such as a "climate crisis" or a "virus pandemic."

The free press has practically been bought out and is controlled and misused as a Ministry of Propaganda, and freedom of expression is steadily being eroded. There is just one 'correct route' in every policy field; dissident opposition is demonized, scorned, or silenced. Dissident voices are vilified, mocked, or silenced. 'Wrong' politicians and public figures are subjected to show trials, excluded, fired or sidelined in other ways.

We're dealing with a government that wants more power and is gaining it through more taxes and regulations, as well as a slew of additional requirements that stifle privacy and the freedom to self-determination. Furthermore, it imposes more harsh consequences on those who reject, and therefore begins to act like a terrorist organization. The judiciary only acts as a'stamp of approval' for government policy, much like it did in the communist Eastern Bloc. The'separation of powers' is no longer an issue, thus citizens and small businesses have no prospect of winning a court lawsuit against the government.

A critical blunder: money is concentrated in a small elite group.

The connection to the fall of the Roman Empire is more than valid for all of these reasons. Total corruption was celebrated high tide in Rome, as it is still, and it was "party on" and "business as usual" until the very end. Money could not stop depreciating, and life became increasingly oriented on ever flatter and more endless pleasure, fun, and enjoyment. Nobody seemed to see that the empire was decaying from the inside. As a result, the Empire, once thought to be invincible, might implode and dissolve in a matter of days before finally falling.

In terms of the grim picture for our civilization, 'The Fourth Turning' is far from unique. NASA's Goddard Space Center financed a research project led by mathematician Safa Motesharrei six years ago (National Socio-Environmental Synthesis Center). They likened Western advancements to those of the Roman, Han, Maurya, Gupta, and Mesopotamian civilizations.

They determined that in the last 5,000 years, no highly developed, complex, or creative civilization has been able to sustain itself indefinitely, and that the West, too, is on the verge of extinction. The major reason is that, like every other civilisation before it, the West appears to have made the critical error of not properly sharing rising wealth throughout society.

The vast majority of money, particularly during the 1990s, has been concentrated in the hands of a small elite minority (primarily in the financial, economic, and political sectors), despite the fact that it is produced by the poorer masses. The poorest people, on the other hand, are oblivious to it.

This imbalance leads to a 'type L' collapse, in which ordinary people are unable to make ends meet as a result of the increased burden, and they become impoverished and hungry. Governments, as is customary everywhere, respond with increased control and repression, oppressing and terrorizing their citizens. Massive popular uprisings, revolutions, and civil wars then follow, sometimes slowly, sometimes quickly, in which civilians seek vengeance on the elite.

Deagel and the MIT computer model

In addition to 'The Fourth Turning' and NASA studies, the famed Massachusetts Institute of Technology's (MIT) 'World One' computer model, developed in 1973 and continuously updated subsequently, predicted the collapse of civilisation between 2020 and 2040.

Several articles have appeared in recent years about Deagel, an American private non-profit military intelligence website that predicts the disappearance of hundreds of millions of people in Europe and America between now and 2025 as a result of a total collapse of the economy, prosperity, and society based on data from the CIA, the IMF, and the UN.

The unsustainable debt burden that both America and Europe have accumulated, according to Deagel, is the primary culprit, which will finally wipe out our prosperity in a series of severe catastrophes. People who can emigrate will do so, but millions more will perish in the ensuing pandemonium or commit suicide because their safe lifestyles have been destroyed

19

forever. According to Deagel, after the downfall of the West, the center of human civilisation will transfer to Russia and China.

'A probable global epidemic of, say, Ebola or any other virus is not even counted in the figures,' I wrote on August 16, 2018, in a piece titled 'MIT computer model predicts end of prosperity by 2020 and end of civilization by 2040.'

In 2020, a manufactured virus crisis will occur, and the Western elite will seize power.

Is it still possible to avoid the collapse of our civilization? Yes, but that necessitates something that has never been done before in the world, in any era: leaders who retrace their steps, abandon their nepotism, misuse of power, and greed culture, and restore prosperity and freedom to the people. Furthermore, they must take responsibility for their (mis)actions and be willing to suffer the consequences. Take a look at The Hague, Brussels, Berlin, Paris, Rome, and Washington: do you believe this will happen?

This year, the Western elite has used an ordinary flu-like coronavirus to carry out a final coup d'état that is unique in human history in order to avert a new global banking and debt catastrophe. Never before have political leaders oppressed their own citizens to such an extent, forbidding and criminalizing regular human contact and destroying the welfare and prosperity of hundreds of millions of people around the world.

According to various estimates, the number of deaths caused by the Corona policy - including large numbers of untreated or late-treated patients with heart disease, tumors, brain hemorrhages, diabetes, etc., as well as people who starve to death or commit suicide - is already a multiple of the official number of Covid deaths, which is likely at least ten times higher due to proven data falsification. The ruling forces, on the other hand, see this as a necessary sacrifice for the 'Big Reset,' which is being carried out under the communist UN Agenda 21/30.

Only a large peaceful rebellion will be able to overthrow the totalitarian control system.

This 'cabal' of politicians and billionaires will attempt to avert inevitable popular uprisings in the coming years by combining mandatory social distancing (1.5 meters) with cutting-edge technology (hundreds of billions of cameras and sensors, thousands of satellites, 5G, DNA-altering vaccines), as well as violent repression by police and military, to establish an unprecedented totalitarian state.

What can nations do to prevent such a horrible future for themselves and their (grand)children? The only solution is to use the power of numbers: peacefully rise up in large groups; decide by the millions to stop cooperating with the measures. A significant percentage of the corporate community, as well as the police and military, support the people.

Violence is never a solution; it simply leads to more violence and forceful intervention, which leads to more bloodshed. Only when a government (whether an occupying regime or one's own) turns to terrorism and begins violently arresting, imprisoning, and disposing of citizens in 'facilities' (internment/concentration camps, prisons, and so on) without any form of trial and/or on the basis of illegal laws is violence justified.

When raids are carried out, people are hauled from their houses and taken away, and cops and military start shooting live ammunition in the streets, you will know that this moment has arrived, and we have once again become BEZET territory, which we fervently pray will never occur. Then you have the right, as well as the obligation, to defend yourself and your loved ones.

Do you believe in doomsday scenarios?

You may dismiss the above bleak scenarios as apocalyptic scenarios. At least in the past, the majority of the populace has usually reacted in this way to warnings and signals of impending calamity.

This is why history repeats itself over and over, and humanity rarely, if ever, appears to learn from its mistakes. People and civilizations have repeatedly refused to acknowledge that prosperity and freedom are not givens, that they must be fought for on a daily basis, and that if we do not do so, if we prefer to be preoccupied with materialism and entertainment, power-hungry people will always win, ushering in a new era of misery and oppression.

Why are we so unwilling to learn from history? Because we fail to acknowledge that history is cyclical rather than linear. Because, arrogant as we are, we refuse to consider the idea that history may repeat itself at any time. That is why it repeats itself in EXACTLY THE SAME MANNER - over and over again. Again, it's headed in the wrong way at a breakneck speed, and we're to blame. Those who refuse to see this may deserve nothing more than the totalitarian dictatorship that is currently being imposed on us all.

Chapter 2: Economic suicide in Europe?

New euro crisis could have been prevented - 'People must face the worst-case scenario: everything is in the gutter.'

Companies go bankrupt, and start pulling other companies with them. By September, 50% of the hospitality industry is in danger of falling over, because one and a half meters is not going to work for them, because you can't survive with only half of your customers. 'Taxes are not being adjusted, they are being deferred,' Hulleman begins. 'It turns out that state aid is counted as turnover, on which taxes have to be paid. Entrepreneurs are being caught up left, right, back and front. So the crisis has begun.'

Wellens found out shortly after the 2008 crisis that 'tax money is just being chipped away at bailing out billionaires, the banks. Why would you do that? That's why in 2015 he started the Peuro initiative, together with Jort Kelder and Thierry Baudet, to get a parliamentary inquiry into the euro and the functioning of the eurozone.

It did not come, nor were any daring choices made to prevent a new euro crisis. This could have been done by leaving the euro, or abolishing the euro, or reducing it, and accepting that many problem debts will never be paid off, and could therefore have been written off.

No one in Europe should have any doubts about the sacred euro project.

There is a stipulation in the ESM (European Stability Mechanism) signed by the Netherlands, which can include € 700 billion, that if a financial difficulty emerges in the eurozone, the director of that fund can call the Netherlands, and we must then pay any demanded amount within 7 days.

This was dubbed the "euro gospel" by Arno Wellens, and it was also the title of one of his books. If you bring it up in a neutral discussion with members of parliament, you will be barred from doing so. 'How dare you question the holy euro project,' for example. "While it is the greatest threat to European citizens ever," Hulleman says. It has been dubbed the greatest economic decision in European history by Jort Kelder, yet it is forbidden to be discussed. After all, why not? Because it's incorrect.'

The voter is constantly misled about the fact that it is primarily the banks that want to have this mechanism in place because they want to know that they will always be rescued by the ECB (i.e., with taxpayer money). "However, the objective, unbiased question of how to proceed with the euro cannot be answered," Wellens says. As a result, they muddle through until the next crisis, which is already underway. Then there's an argument.

Corona is to blame for the world's worst economic disaster ever.

Since 2015, we've been in the midst of the "deepest crisis ever." The corona virus was only the catalyst. Unemployment in Spain is already at 35%, and it is expected to rise to 50% to 60% in the next years, with the rest of Europe following suit.

'The trouble with referendums is that they're dubbed a Putin fabrication,' he sarcastically remarks. 'That's why the last referendum on Ukraine, which was designed to be anti-European, had to be canceled right soon.' But, certainly, you can just ask people if they want the euro. Recognizing that this entails a concession of sovereignty because a central finance minister would be required.'

Economic suicide

'Soon, you'll be able to vote for Belgian, French, and Italian politicians you've never heard of, politicians who will make choices about the European currency, which is held in a large pot and will be utilized for the impoverished (euro) countries... Are those folks aware that they are donating their own money, and that as a result, they will soon be significantly worse off economically?

'The 'New Normal' reminds me of a Planet of the Apes episode.'

The 'new normal,' on the other hand, is anything but normal. 'It's like a Planet of the Apes,' Wellens says. 'A form of semi-dictatorship,' says the author. "You just work at home, don't you?" said those who are pleased to go along with the measures. Yes, you can still say that as a civil official whose pay is being paid as usual.'

'Do we get coffee allowance?' is a topic of conversation among civil servants, as well as many large corporations. Wellens has heard firsthand accounts of this. People who say they used to buy coffee at work but now sit at home and want to know if they may get reimbursed or deduct it from their travel expenses. 'They're bickering about an ice cream with their backs to the sea as a 16-meter-high tidal wave approaches,' Hulleman says.

'Strangulation': The CPB has already admitted that the economy will decline by 25%.

People who are forced to stay at home and whose salaries are not paid at all (though this can never be continued financially for long) should already be considered unemployed. Wellens repeats, 'The new normal is economic suicide.' 'That's not going to work at all; it'll be a strangulation.' One and a half meters will never suffice. Many businesses, including the hospitality industry, cannot survive if just 1/6, or even half, of their clients and consequently turnover are present.

Because of the months of (full or partial) closure, many more enterprises will go bankrupt, causing irreparable economic and social devastation throughout the EU. As a result, subsequent unemployment will be massive.

We would have had a fresh banking and euro crisis even if Corona hadn't happened. Corona has merely accelerated the issue a little. Because nothing was fixed after the 2008 crisis, and nothing was fixed after the bank-follow-up crisis in 2015, the next catastrophe would be 'twice as terrible.' In the summer of 2019, Wellens was allowed to warn the House of Representatives about this for the third time, but it was dismissed once more.

'This catastrophe is more severe than the economic crisis that occurred during World War II,' he said. 'We've reached the level of the Weimar Republic.' We'd have to halve the mess (debts, etc.), so we'd have to cancel all mortgages, forfeit debts and receivables, and start over. Yes, a lot of people will become enraged.'

While a fire has already broken out at the front door, the EU is acting like numerous inhabitants of a housing complex squabbling about who should pay for the fire extinguishers, which system they should choose, and how it should be funded.

Chapter 3: Hyperinflation in the US?

The pandemic hoax has sunk the West deeper into debt than WW2 - Britain's largest pension fund (number six in the world) tells investors that withdrawing money might take up to 95 days, and warns of possible insolvency - the United States predicts hyperinflation in the near future.

Most people seems to believe it is normal for central banks to continue producing enormous quantities of money out of thin air at the touch of a button, so that governments can continue spending large sums of money while maintaining their purchasing power. Anyone who has taken two economics classes in high school knows that this is against all financial and fiscal laws, and it will result in a play sooner or later. It's almost here: the Bank of America has officially declared HYPERinflation. This means that the currency's value will plummet, and the cost of most products and services would skyrocket.

According to annual data, the number of US businesses reporting (high) inflation has climbed by about 800%. As a result, Bank of America can't help but conclude that this "at the very least signals that 'temporary' hyperinflation is on the way." Commodities (+28%), consumer prices (+36%), transportation (+35%), and manufactured products, in particular, are on the verge of bursting in price. Despite the BoA's belief that it will remain 'manageable,' hyperinflation is a process that inherently demonstrates that something is spinning out of control.

Exorbitant prices

This means that, among other things, citizens will soon have to pay significantly more for almost everything, and at a far faster rate. In fact, we can already see this disguised high inflation in the increasing property prices (after all, these are not associated with a strong economic recovery, but with a government-funded debt economy). Furthermore, an increasing number of consumers are complaining that their weekly shopping have grown significantly more expensive in a short period of time.

The end of prosperity is approaching.

As distressing as it may be to read, the end of Western affluence is now in sight. Indeed, Europe's predicament is not dissimilar to that of the United States, and in some ways is more worse. Consider Italy's, Greece's, and Spain's, as well as France and Belgium's, never-ending sovereign debts. Furthermore, large European systemic banks such as Deutsche Bank, Société Générale, and UniCredit are basically bankrupt on a technical level.

The New Green Deal and the Great Reset

The EU's "Green Deal" and the World Economic Forum's "Great Reset" are on top of it. The former will make energy, transportation, and food nearly unaffordable for millions of people, while the latter will permanently eliminate the last vestiges of freedom and self-determination we have left, putting 35 percent to 41 percent of people out of work, according to the World Economic Forum's own figures.

And, while the West is tearing itself apart as it realizes the gravity of the situation, China and Russia have already begun to take the lead.

31

Chapter 4: Fuel and food shortage?

Is this the final warm-up for the West's upcoming big cyberattack?

According to experts, the cyber attack on the US's main fuel pipeline could have been resolved in a matter of hours, and thus bears all the hallmarks of a "false flag" operation designed to bring the American people completely to their knees before the emerging communist UN/WEF climate-vaccine dictatorship. The first gas stations have run out of fuel, and those that remain are boosting their prices dramatically. For a long period, fuel may be rationed, and once that is the case, food will surely follow.

According to one IT expert, the Colonial Pipeline from Houston, Texas, to Linden, New Jersey, could have been up and running in a matter of hours if broken gear had been rapidly replaced, since most computer servers nowadays are Virtual Machines (VMs). The outage would have just been minutes long if only the software had been damaged. As a result, the pipeline had many backups in every way.

Because no recovery was indicated until the end of the week, this IT expert believes that the fuel shortages are occurring at random. Diesel is still used in trucks, but only for a limited time. The supermarkets will quickly empty if things come to a halt today or tomorrow, threatening absolute fear and pandemonium. The country will be at a standstill in a week, the drinking water supply will be jeopardized in two weeks, and civilization will be over in four weeks.

North Carolina's governor has proclaimed a state of emergency and has temporarily (?) rationed gasoline. The pumps of major businesses such as Shell and BP are now facing supply issues as well.

Are you whining? Not if you voted for this system in the first place.

Left-wing voters, in particular, should have no complaints, because these parties - like almost all left-wing opposition parties, by the way - openly support the Great Reset / Build Back Better / Agenda-21/2030 agenda and have been working tirelessly for many years to bring this future to you and your (grand)children.

Except for themselves, because, like in previous communist and fascist dictatorships in the past, the power elite will ensure that they are never affected by their own rock-hard freedom and wealth-destroying laws.

Chapter 5: It will take one cyber-attack?!

In 2021-2022, a long-planned new all-digital system, a communist-fascist technocracy, will be formed on the wreckage of the current system.

Klaus Schwab's World Economic Forum will 'simulate' a large cyber-attack in the summer, much as a 'real' exercise with a corona pandemic (Event 201) was held in October 2019 and then carried out three months later. Cyber Polygon 2021 will take place on July 9, 2021, and will serve as a detailed script for what will happen later (possibly as early as the fall): a massive 'attack' on the digital and energy infrastructure, which will bring the West, in particular, to its knees once and for all before the Great Reset.

Why are the Russians taking part in this?

It's unclear who will be held responsible for this heinous false flag operation. The obvious one is the tried-and-true argument that "the Russians did it!" Sberbank, Russia's largest state-owned bank, is participating in Cyber Polygon 2021 with its cyber business BIZONE.

So, what exactly is going on here? Is Russia a part of the World Economic Forum's scheme to bring the West to its knees once and for all? Or are the Russians taking part in Cyber Polygon 2021 because top US politicians and military leaders have openly threatened Russia with a cyber strike for years? If such is the case, it would be prudent to get as knowledgeable as possible about the enemy's tactics so that you can defend yourself.

In 2021-2022, there will be a financial mega-crisis.

As explained in the previous chapters, the inevitable financial mega-crisis has been predicted for years, because the Western - and particularly European - banking system is technically bankrupt, the rapidly growing debt has become unsustainable, the euro has only paper value, and the ECB's years of negative interest rates have completely eroded savings, pensions, and purchasing power of the euro. As a result, we are living 'on borrowed time,' or, to put it another way, time bought with massive quantities of new digital money (tens of billions every month), which has only served to postpone the big blow (and which, partly because of this, will be much harder, and will probably be a fact in 2021-2022).

Because the major systemic crisis is so close, governments, banks, and big financial players need a scapegoat for their planned "false flag" strike, which will deal a "controlled" final blow to the ailing system before it collapses on its own. The devastation caused by the collapse will be so massive, with so many victims, that hundreds of millions of desperate people will want to vent their frustrations on the true perpetrators, in this case the same governments and banks, led by large globalist organizations, with the World Economic Forum at the helm.

Who is going to be the scapegoat?

It is 'essential' to assign a scapegoat to the public in order to avert upheavals and revolutions. Perhaps another group of Russian, Chinese, or Eastern European hackers will be involved. China could be ideal for the United States, as the Pentagon is planning a 'hot' war against it in the near future. Iran and North Korea may also be cited, maybe collaborating with China to form a new 'axis of evil,' which would then have to be 'naturally' fought.

Is the hatred with China only a ruse designed to stoke public fears of war and other disasters? After all, both the US and the EU are attempting to replicate China's authoritarian control regime.

Another possibility is that the false flag cyber assault is traced to Israel, which NATO and the UN Security Council will exploit to compel the military-threatened country to accept to a "peace plan" that will split the country in two and turn Jerusalem into some kind of international capital. The Vatican and Freemasonry have had their sights set on Jerusalem for a long time, as we demonstrated in various articles more than ten years ago, since they want to make it the hub of some kind of unified new world religion.

In any case, the corona pandemic hoax has demonstrated unambiguously that it must be presented as insane or unlikely in order for the vastly misinformed, indifferent, and drunk Western public to believe it. EVERYTHING governments and the media claim is now accepted as fact because "it was broadcast on TV, so it must be true."

A communist-fascist technocracy in which your own body is no longer yours.

Since last year, the World Economic Forum's Great Reset has been breaking down and dramatically changing our society. The last vestiges of liberty, democracy, and self-determination will vanish forever, cash will be replaced by fully digital currencies, and the new'stakeholder capitalism' will be nothing more than a combined communist-fascist system in which citizens and businesses will lose everything, including the right to control their own bodies.

The government effectively becomes the sole major shareholder in almost every facet of life. Because this system allows for the introduction of a Universal Basic Income, and because the aforementioned planned cyber-attack would bring so much confusion and agony, people will accept any remedy without question, even with tremendous excitement. ("Ordo ab Chao") is a Latin phrase that means "order of the gods."

However, the survivors of the impending global crisis will soon discover that they have no power and no say in the new system, not even over their own bodies. They will become genetically altered digital slaves, a

37

form of androids or cyborgs, as a result of one forced mRNA vaccination after another - potentially soon carrying nano-chips. Klaus Schwab has practically proclaimed the implementation of forced brain scans and chips that can control and alter your thoughts, desires, and willpower.

The World Economic Forum is endangering humanity's survival; hence, a true Great Reset is required.

As a result, the World Economic Forum clearly identifies itself as one of the greatest threats to humanity's survival. It is possible that the World Economic Forum, with the help of Western powers, may go a long way, but we anticipate that this heinous anti-human regime will not survive long. They believe they can control and change human nature because of their limitless arrogance, but what they will create is nothing short of hell on Earth, which will consume itself under the weight of its own megalomaniac malignancy.

Then, according to believers, it will be time for a true Great Reset, which will be carried out "from on high." That kingdom of peace will continue forever, and Klaus Schwab, Bill Gates, George Soros, and Mark Zuckerberg, as well as the banking elite still above them, commanded by the famed Rothschild family, will no longer be welcome. That "Babylon" will be demolished for all time, never to rise again to torment humanity.

The arrival of a new Great Depression is simply a matter of time.

We would be in a worse Depression now than in the 1930s if half of the economy had not been put on a drip since last year. So it's a good solution, right? Try to recall your first economics lesson in high school, or the question that almost every child has asked their parents at some point why we don't just put money in the copy machine so that we always have enough and can get "rich."

Banks need to be bailed out again

No one is talking about the need to reduce debt anymore. All parties - governments and businesses - hope that interest rates will remain zero or negative forever, and money will continue to play no role for the state. Indeed, the absolute horror scenario is a rise in interest rates. Even if it is small, that will immediately push two even much larger European debt states, Italy and Spain, into state bankruptcy. Rescue is out of the question, as it would cost trillions of euros. Therefore, the collapse of either of these two countries immediately means the collapse of the eurozone.

'Contributions to sanitation,' but from whom?

As a result, the IMF advises governments to impose 'clean-up payments' on incomes, assets, and earnings - an odd advice given that only strong and sustained economic development can possibly pull us back from the verge of a systemic collapse. If you then impose even higher taxes on an already struggling economic sector, you will only have the opposite effect: the crisis will be accelerated and intensified, hundreds of thousands of businesses will fail, and countless people will lose their jobs.

And there is nothing more to be obtained from a population that is already strained. Even higher taxes and worse cuts will engulf significant swaths of the lower and middle classes in abject poverty. Governments have little choice but to use draconian financial repression, which will hurt the average citizen, but particularly the poor and vulnerable.

Millions of people may soon be unable to pay for basic necessities such as housing, energy, and foodstuffs. The majority of us will have to figuratively and literally tighten our belts.

Some analysts predict "Weimar"-style hyperinflation, which will wipe out our purchasing power totally. However, given the current vulnerable circumstances of many residents and businesses, even a far lower inflation rate of 3% to 4% will be the ultimate blow. In short time, government bonds, life insurance plans, pension funds, and savings will be worthless.

The world's sixth largest insurer has issued a 'insolvency' warning.

Signs that the financial system crisis is getting closer are also obvious in the United Kingdom, where Aviva, the country's largest insurer/pension fund and the world's sixth, has notified its customers that withdrawing money from their accounts might take up to 95 days.

The actual warning that "in the improbable event that we become insolvent... " is much more frightening. If a bank, insurer, or pension fund employs that word at all, it's a sign that they're dealing with exceedingly serious, and most likely unsolvable issues.

Gold, silver and cash removed from Great Britain

A large sum of gold, silver, and cash was abruptly withdrawn from the United Kingdom and transferred to Qatar early last week, with no explanation. A payment of $1.8 billion from the Hillary Clinton Foundation to the Qatari Central Bank was recorded by the Bank of International Settlements (the BIS bank in Basel, the "central bank of central banks") (QCB).

Possible theories range from the United Kingdom's impending financial collapse to a future conflict with Russia in which British cities could be annihilated with nuclear weapons.

Citizens and businesses will own nothing in the digital euro.

We've been warning for years that a systemic crisis is on the way, and it appears to be approaching. The 'Great Reset,' which is nothing more than the establishment of an unprecedentedly harsh and oppressive technocratic communist climate-vaccine dictatorship, will be used to push through the 'Great Reset,' which will be triggered under the guise of a false flag cyber-attack (supposedly by Russia?).

In financial and economic terms, this means that the euro will be totally digital, that everything (even your own body) will be controlled by the government, and that citizens and businesses will be forever bereft of any kind of property or say in the issue. The World Economic Forum also expects a permanent unemployment rate of 35 to 41 percent, as well as the implementation of a basic income that is just enough to keep people alive.

You want this WEF reset? Then you'll get it.

This is what will happen, and it will not be stopped. Even if the majority of people were to wake up at the last minute and revolt against it, a 'Great Reset' would still be required, but of a completely different magnitude than the WEF and globalists in Washington, Brussels, London, Paris, Berlin, Rome, and The Hague. Their reset concentrates all power and riches in a tiny group of people, whilst the Reset that we actually need achieves the exact opposite.

The technically bankrupt Deutsche Bank has warned that the EU's 'Green Deal,' which is supposed to enable the 'Great Reset,' will instead trigger a mega-crisis and usher in an eco-dictatorship that will destroy our current affluence.

Chapter 6: The next world war?

The West made a catastrophic error in expecting that Russia would only deploy nuclear weapons at the last possible moment.

The United States Strategic Command (USSTRATCOM) has released a report claiming that the unpredictability of nuclear war is now officially considered. 'Today's conflict spectrum is neither linear nor predictable. We must consider the potential that a confrontation could fast lead to circumstances that might prompt an adversary to use nuclear weapons as a last resort.' What the US fails to recognize is that Russia will not wait for a conventional war to end before resorting to nuclear weapons.

Surprisingly, NATO continues to believe that Russia is incapable of winning a war. In believing so, NATO makes the major fallacy that the Russians will first try to repel a Western attack by conventional means, and only when they are in danger of losing that battle will they turn to nuclear weapons.

This military doctrine is mostly founded on a mix of unbridled hubris about military superiority no longer existent in reality and a complete lack of comprehension of Russian mentality (and Chinese as well). President Vladimir Putin, on the other hand, was very explicit when he told a news conference a few years ago that one thing he learned on the street is that when you're cornered and a fight is imminent, the best thing to do is deliver the first blow yourself.

Hundreds of thousands of troops are pitted against one another.

Near Luhansk and Donetsk (the Donbass), Ukraine has gathered 110,000 men, along with 450 tanks and 800 pieces of artillery. Another 40,000 NATO troops are stationed in the nations surrounding Ukraine. Last Monday, the United States began transferring tanks, fighter jets, and other weaponry to the future battleground.

There are 150,000 to 200,000 Russian troops, 1,300 tanks, 1,300 pieces of artillery, 380 multiple rocket launchers, 300 fighter planes and bombers, 3,700 drones, 280 helicopters, 26 ships, and 4,000+ armored vehicles deployed across a 1,000-kilometer front. By the way, these weren't transferred to the front lines until Ukraine dispatched tens of thousands of troops to the Donbass and President Zelensky signed a paper demanding the capture of Crimea, which was essentially a declaration of war against Russia.

Clearly, the Kremlin has drawn a line after years of steely patience and many overtures at reconciliation— all of which were repeatedly rejected by the West. It will not give up Crimea, will not allow Ukraine to launch another war against Russian citizens in the Donbass, and will not accept the NordStream II gas pipeline to

Germany not being completed. The Americans intend to deprive Russia of its profits and force the Europeans to buy their far more expensive LNG as a result of their typical blackmail tactics.

If it comes to war, Ukraine will not stand a chance against Russia. Only if NATO and the US subsequently decide not to intervene under any circumstances will a Third World War still be prevented.

The West acts "like a drug-addled Santa Claus."

Attempting to impose even more sanctions on Russia has historically yielded no results. The Russian economy has continued to expand, and this has brought Russians and Chinese closer together. As a result, Margarita Simonyan, the chief of Russian state media, compared Western American-led behavior to "a kind of manic Santa Claus who is on antidepressants or drugs."

Attempting to impose even more sanctions on Russia has historically yielded no results. The Russian economy has continued to expand, and this has brought Russians and Chinese closer together. As a result, Margarita Simonyan, the chief of Russian state media, compared Western American-led behavior to "a kind of manic Santa Claus who is on antidepressants or drugs."

Chapter 7: Blatant lies

U.S. Air Force summit leaves F-35 out of simulations as defeat is assured.

While Russia and Ukraine test their nuclear bunkers to see if they are still operational in the event of a nuclear war, the Western media and public continue to believe that ignorance is bliss. Many people, especially (ex) military personnel, assume that America and NATO will simply "win a war" with Russia and/or China. Forget it, declares Scott Ritter, a 'retired'* American intelligence officer who served on General Schwarzkopf's staff during the Gulf War and as an INF and UN weapons inspector in the (former) Soviet Union.

According to him, American superiority is built solely on "lies and self-deception. Even in simulations, the West can only win a war if there is blatant cheating.

The US Air Force conducted "war exercises" in 2018 and 2019 to see if it could protect Taiwan against a Chinese invasion. In both situations, the United States was soundly defeated. The same simulation was held in 2020, and America prevailed, but only by fabricating vast capabilities like non-existent airfields and command centers, as well as aircraft that are only on the drawing board or have yet to be invented. "This experiment was as far off from reality as one could get," Ritter added. 'The truth is that the United States can only defend Taiwan against China in its dreams.'

47

The most expensive European defense project is the "Wreck of the Sky."

Surprisingly, the F-35, which is also replacing the F-16 in Europe, was not even deployed virtually in the most recent simulation because top US Air Force brass judged that the aircraft is completely incapable of winning a battle in a war. (In all simulations, the F-35s were 'shot out of the sky like flies,' according to a Pentagon officer a few years ago.)

And this 'wreck of the sky' was purchased by the Europe for €6 billion, our most expensive defense project ever. Good luck with it, or rather: good luck, should it indeed come to a war with Russia, as the Western globalists seem to have wanted for so long.

'Deaths sold as victories, lies packaged as truths'

Ritter illustrates that American air superiority, and thus battlefield superiority, has long been a thing of the past. People's thoughts are still flooded with pictures from the first Gulf War in 1991, but the situation currently is incomparable. Following 9/11, the US military switched its focus from winning "big" conventional battles with Russia and China to the "war on terror" and "country building" (which in reality became "nation destruction" everywhere).

Even the extraordinarily expensive wars in Afghanistan, Iraq, and Syria were difficult to win in the end. 'By failing to win, the US lost the 'forever wars' in the Middle East and Southeast Asia. As a result, the US military's senior brass has been conditioned to view failure as a foregone conclusion, which is explained away by lying to themselves, their superiors, or both. Too many successful professions are founded on lies masquerading as truths, setbacks masquerading as successes, and flaws masquerading as assets.'

In a word, that is the Western worldview in many sectors, not just military. It is an ever louder warning signal that our civilization has turned against itself through corruption, lust for power, greed for money and nepotism, and is hearing deaf and seeing blind to its own demise.

Only nuclear weapons can stop the US from fighting China or Russia.

In many ways, the recently concluded US Air Force 'war game' is a by-product of this psychosis - a self-deception exercise in which reality has been replaced by a fictional world in which everything works as planned, even if it doesn't exist. The US Air Force is currently unable to wage a successful war against China or Russia. Its ability to successfully conduct an air campaign against Iran or North Korea is also in doubt. This is the kind of truth that would lose a lot of senior individuals their jobs - with or without uniforms - in a world where facts still mattered.'

'However, because the culpability for this general incompetence is so extensive, no genuine accountability for what occurred is imaginable.' Instead, when confronted with the truth of its flaws, the US Air Force 'invents' victory. This 'win' is meaningless in and of itself. If China invaded Taiwan, the United States would have no choice but to use nuclear weapons to stop them.'

'Behavior pattern based on falsehoods, deception, and self-deception'

The planned acquisition of additional aircraft, according to Ritter, are based only on these fabrications, on this false notion of an air force that can 'win' wars.

The United States Air Force is just repeating a pattern of behavior based on falsehoods, deception, and self-delusion that it has allowed to lead it for the past two decades, including top officers and political leaders. The eventual effect will be that, even if the US Air Force is given all of the resources and capabilities required to "defend" and win Taiwan in a war simulation (which it will not be), the only place they will win is in their dreams.'

A nuclear war will also be lost by the West.

Even if the Americans resort to nuclear weapons, according to American radio personality and former intelligence official Hal Turner, the fight will be lost. He cites the fact that Russia has constructed massive shelters for its citizens, in which millions of people may survive for extended periods of time. The United States, like the Europe, has no such shelters.

Chapter 8: China joins the game

"In 4 weeks, a World War might be unleashed in Ukraine as Putin sends 4,000 troops and tanks to the border," The Sun, Britain's most famous tabloid newspaper, recently headlined.

Whether it causes a stir or not, the announcement that China would soon send 5,000 troops to Iran is extremely dangerous. Furthermore, Tehran demonstrated a cruise missile capable of hitting Berlin, and the mullahs guaranteed their support for Russia in the event that Ukraine launched a frontal attack on Crimea and the Donbass, sparking a NATO-led war.

Only a "psychoanalyst" can understand Moscow's aims, according to Russian military analyst Pavel Felgenhauer, who also warned that developments might lead to a catastrophic war within a month.

All the sorrow brought upon by the coup in 2014

In 2014, the CIA orchestrated a violent coup in Ukraine with the help of the US and EU. The country's democratically elected president was toppled and replaced with a Western-backed puppet dictatorship, which launched a murderous war against the country's Russian-speaking populace in the east.

In order to bring Ukraine into NATO as quickly as possible, a highly probable "false flag" attack was carried out on a passenger plane (MH17) flying from Amsterdam to Malaysia, which was deliberately directed by Ukrainian air traffic control over war zones.

Russia's major naval port in Sevastopol (Crimea) would be lost, and once NATO bases are erected in Ukraine, Russia's nuclear weapons could be destroyed by American missiles in a surprise attack in minutes, putting the country defenseless.

China dispatches 5000 troops to Iran, which has launched a missile capable of striking Berlin.

However, an axis is forming that is fed up with years of American-led Western racism and war-mongering, as well as all those ostensibly "peace and democracy" missions that have murdered millions of people just this century. The Islamic Republic of Iran, for example, unveiled a new cruise missile with a range of 3,000 kilometers capable of hitting Berlin last Saturday.

Meanwhile, China has announced significant billion-dollar expenditures in Iran, including the deployment of 5,000 troops and the establishment of new military outposts.

Is the West's already-disappeared light going out for good?

In January 2018, the BBC in the United Kingdom aired a simulated news program about the start of a war between NATO and Russia, with nuclear weapons being launched after only one hour. A similar fictitious announcement of World War III with Russia was broadcast by the German public broadcaster.

Call it scaremongering or predictive programming, but one thing is clear at the start of 2021: in recent years, we have only had leaders, media, and institutions in the West, as well as in our own country, who can only lie and cheat coldly about important issues, whether it is about Russia, the coronavirus, vaccinations, or the climate. The light, like their leaders, has long since vanished for those who fall for this with their eyes open and/or sometimes even think it's a good thing. Worse, what was previously light has been renamed darkness, and what was darkness has been renamed light.

Russia, China, and Iran are all under fire, but it's unclear how much time the West has left to come to its senses, look in the mirror, and admit how far we've fallen as a so-called advanced 'civilization.' If we keep going at our current rate, it won't be more than 10 years or so, and if The Sun is correct for once, it won't be more than 10 weeks. When this more likely catastrophe occurs, it will be unexpected for the vast majority of us, and totally our own responsibility, in our opinion.

Chapter 9: The West against Russia

'Extremely serious threat to national security' is only one step away from declaring war.

Because of the "unique and unprecedented threat that Russia represents to the national security, foreign policy, and economics of the United States," US President Joe Biden has proclaimed a "state of national emergency." The United States is expelling ten Russian diplomats and implementing new restrictions. Russia is intensively preparing its army and fleet for a great (global) conflict, which it worries - and rightfully so - that the increasingly aggressive Americans are out to start.

The only people who stood in the way of the Western globalists' "Great Reset" were Trump and Putin. Trump was exonerated thanks to the largest election fraud in history; now it's Russia's turn. America's and Europe's mad neo-Marxist technocrats seemed to believe they can win a war against Russia without causing too much damage.

Russia is preparing for war.

As a result, Russia will expel a large number of American diplomats. The Kerch Strait, which connects the Crimean peninsula and the Russian mainland, will be closed to all navy and foreign-owned boats starting next week.

The closure will last until October, and mainly affects the Ukrainian port cities of Mariupol and Berdyansk.

Near the Ukrainian border, Russian armored vehicles and trucks were spotted with so-called "invasion stripes." Clear white stripes are painted on the vehicles to protect them from being shot down by their own planes and tanks. This appears to signal that Russia is really considering putting an end to the Western-backed Neo-Nazi administration in Kiev, which, as our readers are aware, has been attempting for years to create a massive NATO-Russia war.

Ukraine claims that more than 110,000 Russian troops, 330 airplanes, and 240 helicopters will be stationed along its border. Kiev alleges that Russia is transferring nuclear weapons to Crimea, but we have our doubts. Indeed, Russia is under no obligation to do so; Ukraine could theoretically be annihilated by nuclear weapons launched from anywhere on the planet.

The majority of the Russian Pacific Fleet has returned to Vladivostok and is being properly resupplied there, according to satellite pictures. At least one naval warship is receiving "new" missiles on board. This suggests that Russia expects any conflict to go beyond Ukraine and into the rest of the world.

It appears that a military clash between the US and Russia is only a matter of time.

Now that the US president has branded Russia a "danger to national security," and Biden has given the command to respond to that "threat," the military clash that Washington and Brussels have long desired appears to be only a matter of time, potentially just a few weeks away.

President Putin has long recognized how the West operates and, as a result, has turned down the offer of a meeting with Vice President Joe Biden. This would be nothing more than the world-famous Western blackmail diplomacy ('we want peace, but only on our terms, and if you don't agree, our bombs and missiles will follow'), which has claimed the lives of millions of people in the last two decades alone.

'The war-mongering neocons are doing exactly what they had to stop doing in 2016 when Trump's victory shattered their satanic preparations for war with Russia... Then there were many who claimed Trump was dangerous,' says Hall Turner, an American radio presenter. 'This senile demented half-wit is going to be the ruin of us all,' says Biden.

We presumably don't need to explain what this says about the mental state of European leaders, who were so shocked when this warmongering 'half-wit' managed to wrestle the Trump they despised out of the White House, nor do they appear to care what happens to you, me, and hundreds of millions of other people.

Chapter 10: Agenda 21 summarized

'The nation state, freedom, and your voice are all being suffocated.' - 'Only mass resistance will be able to stop this anti-human plan from being enacted.'

Café Weltschmerz has published an interview with a well-known top American expert on Agenda 21, which can be summarized as a power grab that will eventually subjugate the entire world to a technocratic communist dictatorship in which individuals and peoples will have no say whatsoever, including over their own health and lives. The next phase of this de facto coup against our freedom, democracy, and right to self-determination has begun with the Covid-19 fear pandemic deception.

Café Weltschmerz does not post "The hidden aim underlying the downfall of our society" under it for nothing - damage that is being carried out on purpose by the European government as well.

Rosa Koire, the executive director of the Post Sustainability Institute and an expert on land use and property rights who has given speeches all over the world, was interviewed by independent journalist Spiro Kouras (Activist Post). Democrats United Against UN Agenda21, a website that was inaccessible at the time of writing, has a collection of her work.

Koire is also the author of "Behind the Green Mask: The United Nations Agenda 21." In 1992, 178 countries, including the Vatican, endorsed Agenda 21. A globalist power elite seeks total control of all land, water, vegetation, minerals, construction, means of production, food, and energy with this purpose. This total control must extend to law enforcement, education, information, and the people themselves.

Agenda 2030: a first step toward the abolition of the nation-state and freedom

Large sums of "money" must also be transferred from developed to developing countries. In the end, it's about robbing you of your right to have a voice and a representative government. 'National governments devolve into bureaucracies.' Your ability to be free and self-sufficient is being systematically eroded. The idea is to shift authority from local governments and individuals to a global governance structure...

It's a scheme to destabilize and destroy the current system. It's a transformation and control strategy, and that's what we're seeing right now.'

Agenda 2030, like 2020, 2025, and 2050, is merely a step forward in Agenda 21. This nefarious scheme must be accomplished by 2050, with the help and assistance of great globalist personalities like Ford, Rockefeller, Soros, Gates, Zuckerberg, Musk, the Pope, and, last but not least, Rothschild. All nation-states will be eliminated by 2050, with the world's population concentrated in a few megacities that can engulf entire nations and countries (just as the Netherlands, along with Belgium and the German Ruhr, is to become one big city).

'This is intended to suffocate your power to control what happens to you.' It's a worldwide strategy, but it's being implemented in diverse ways around the world.' This is done on purpose to draw people's attention away from the genuine goals.

In truth, Agenda 21 encompasses all that is referred to as "green" or "sustainable development." This includes 'climate change,' which encompasses all climate agreements and efforts, as well as Covid-19. 'A global issue necessitates a global response,' they argue. This requires global governance.'

Climate change and the corona pandemic are "intended to push people into a panic, so bad that you literally worry you won't survive it," according to the authors. According to Koire, whether or not there is a climate problem is irrelevant. It is so effective that it would have been invented regardless (indeed, it IS invented, conceived, in the early 1990s, which is literally written in UN documents).

The 'Great (Green) Reset' is underway.

Skouras then mentions the World Economic Forum's 'Great (Green) Reset,' which was announced at Davos. 'I don't want to sound alarmist,' Koire answers, but she is afraid that this'reset' is now being pushed through regardless of the cost to people and society. They are, however, keeping their Green Masks on since once they are removed, the Army boots and trenches are shown.' Quite literally.

We have now arrived at a position when those in power are unconcerned about the public's protests and worries. 'It's like they're sending us a message that they don't care about us anymore.' Although it appears that there isn't much more we can accomplish, Koire feels that it is still doable.

Technology has progressed to the point where two major goals, eternal life and the ability to construct your own existence, are now within reach. 'These folks have no ethical boundaries, which is quite concerning. You saw it with the Nazis, Stalin, and now with the current administration. There is nothing that can be done to stop these people.'

Everything and everyone will be connected to the internet.

Everything and everyone will be digitally connected in the 'Fourth Industrial Revolution' that they have already set in motion.

They're discussing a new social compact. In most cases, both parties to a contract have something to say about it. However, this is a contract in which neither of us has a voice... One of the causes for the panic in the streets is because of this. This is because it's a warning, a message to us: this is what will happen to you if you take to the streets and defy our plan.'

'People ask me, 'Who is it that is torturing us?' That's the government you're dealing with. The government of your country has been taken over.' An attempt is being made to incite an insurrection with the support of groups and movements such as Antifa and Black Lives Matter.

'We're being attacked.' This was the catalyst for Koire's defection from the Democratic Party. 'However, parties are merely a diversion. Power knows no party at the top. All available means are being deployed in this globalist conquest of power.

The plan is to disrupt and disrupt again, and that is exactly what is happening right now. This is a pretty successful strategy for destroying social cohesion.'

Individual deconstruction is referred to as 'transformation.'

'Transformation' is a commonly used magic word in education, the economy, law enforcement, and society. 'In reality, transformation is about dismantling the individual, of any 'old' structure, such as your family, your 'old' views, or your faith... It's a psychological approach that deconstructs your personality before rebuilding it (according to their new criteria).'

The word "institutional racism" is nothing more than a pretext for destroying your mind. It was employed by Mao Zedong, Sung, and the Nazis. It's a method of dismantling your individuality in order to recreate you as a new human being, a new world citizen.'

A.I. and humans must become one.

Artificial intelligence (A.I.) also plays a role in this process. A (global) A.I. police force is on the way, and it will not be made up of people. Drones will also eventually be controlled by artificial intelligence rather than humans. 'I don't think I need to explain that, because then you're in a really dangerous situation.' In Singapore, intelligent robots are increasingly being used to enforce social separation, while New Zealand recently unveiled its first A.I. police officer.

'This is fundamentally an anti-humanitarian goal, where they want to integrate human and machine (AI) intelligence,' Skouras said.

Everyone has been branded a possible enemy of each other under the Covid-19 measures. The premise is that even your closest family members and friends are no longer trustworthy. At the same time, our health is deteriorating, according to Koire, which is a key component of the Agenda 21 plan. 'This is the government's plan to inventory and control everything, including your DNA (thus the government's insistence that as many people as possible be tested for Covid-19, which will allow your DNA to be extracted and stored immediately).'

You must 'prove' that you are a loyal and obedient citizen who is 'worthy' of continuing to live in the new order based on your 'social credit status,' as in China and soon in the US and Europe. Of course, the system has been doing this for a long time by favoring select brilliant people, who are then forced to pay the price. The Chinese system will be implemented all over the world.

Vaccine for depopulation

'In the 1990s, the Chinese also promised to collaborate with the US on a depopulation vaccine.' Is that something they actually did? Is that vaccine currently available, and is it being'sold' to humankind under a new name (maybe the Covid-19 vaccine?)? 'Depopulation is an integral aspect of the plan,' in any case. You must be 'separated' and relocated if it is found that you do not have enough value and/or are taking up too much space, using too much energy, water, or land.

'This is the crux of the climate change agenda.' The European Union's climate change agenda is all about climate change, and European farmers are well aware of this, as their lives and work are increasingly being made impossible by the European government, which is busy turning all Agenda 21 points into policy, regardless of the cost to our country's prosperity and well-being.

The vast majority of humankind will be forced to live in ('multicultural') megacities, where every element of our life will be monitored and controlled 24 hours a day, 7 days a week, 365 days a year. 'This approach will essentially take away all of your freedom. And this isn't something that will happen in the future; it's something that is already happening. So this isn't something that will happen in 2030 or 2050. 2020 is an extremely significant year. Many of these strategies are already being implemented on a regional scale.'

'Awareness is the first step; action is the second.'

Is it still possible to stop this? 'The first step of resistance is awareness,' explains Koire. 'The second step is to take action.' People need to recognize that we have been socialized to be passive and believe that pressing 'like' on social media means we are politically engaged; but, if you don't leave your house, you are not a political activist. They aim to declare public opposition to Agenda 21's destruction and absolute control plan illegal and impossible in advance, which is why they're enforcing lockdowns and social distance.

'And don't claim that your government is so horrible that you have no recourse.' I'm sure it appears that way, but only because you've allowed it to progress this far. It's not going to get any better if you just ignore it. That is why I believe you should "occupy" your government (lett. occupy, also "seize," "occupy," or "occupy"). Be in charge of your own government. Yes, we are in the last stages of the game, and we don't have much time left. So you should've done it a long time ago.'

People must begin to recognize Agenda 21 in their own communities and regions. It's a good idea to bring it up in your local council. Talk to people's representatives on a regular basis about it. Every item on your city council's agenda is almost certainly tied to Agenda 21. ' She encourages people to visit her website and read her book in order to "learn out how they manage public opinion so you don't cause them difficulties." They want you to sit in your chair at home.'

So get involved, talk to people and officials, distribute flyers, share films, and write and publish about it.' Because simply being aware of the situation and doing nothing about it is no longer sufficient. You must become politically involved and be willing to accept that you will not be able to take over everything from them right away.' They want to begin replacing reality with VR (virtual reality), for example, because it would make living so much more enjoyable. 'However, as soon as you begin doing so, your life will be over.' As a result, you must resist.'

If Wikipedia is to be believed, Agenda 21 is an anti-human agenda.

'Talk about it wherever you work, wherever you go.'
That will irritate a lot of people, and it will irritate you as
well (anymore). But so be it; whether we like it or not,
this plan is genuine and is being implemented right
now.' What Wikipedia claims about Agenda 21 is
incorrect. It is neither voluntary nor 'non-binding.' This
plan is required for you.... So let's band together and
combat this. We must all stand against it.'

'Indeed,' Skouras says. They're pitching it as a way to
better and save the globe, the climate, and the
environment. However, (Plan 21 / 2030) is an anti-
human agenda that is currently being implemented. We
don't want to down that dark road to tyranny.'

Chapter 11: Orchestrated drama

All for the sake of realizing 'Agenda 2030,' a global totalitarian communist government that requires the destruction of Western affluence - The UN High Commissioner for Human Rights does not want lockdowns to end just yet.

In an interview with The Guardian, Lise Kingo, the executive director of the UN'Global Compact, conceded that there are'very, very apparent parallels' between the humanitarian crisis, the 'anti-racism' protests by and for Black Lives Matter, and the climate agenda. According to Kingo, the global response to Corona—lockdowns, social isolation, and the partial destruction of the present economy—is really a "dress rehearsal" for what will happen if a "global climate emergency" is declared.

She cautioned that the Corona situation is only a "fire practice" for what's to come. She said the so-called pandemic, anti-racism protests and climate are all part of the UN's 'sustainable development agenda'. 'The only course forward is by creating a world where no one is disadvantaged.'

The killing of violent felon George Floyd in Minneapolis, according to King, demonstrates that "awful racism" still persists. She went on to say that "human rights" are intrinsically related to the environment. Furthermore, the woman advises large corporations and CEOs to become "social activists," claiming that young people will only work for them if "social equality" is encouraged.

The UN High Commissioner for Human Rights does not want lockdowns to end, even though vaccines are being rolled out

Despite the fact that tens of millions of people have already lost their jobs and the number of estimated deaths from the lockdowns will be 25 times higher than from the coronavirus, Kingo's colleague Michelle Bachelet, High Commissioner for Human Rights, believes the lockdowns should not be lifted 'too quickly.'

Indeed, Bachelet professes to be scared of the "second wave," which, according to a huge number of independent scientists and other experts, will be nothing more than "psy-op" propaganda because the majority of the people is naturally immune to the virus.

The United Nations intends to utilize the corona issue to "tear down the fossil economy."

In April, UN Secretary-General António Guterres urged the West, in particular, to use the sanctions to destabilize the "fossil" economy. Guterres, a born Marxist, sees the financial crisis as a golden opportunity to implement his vision of a worldwide communist tyranny under the United Nations banner ('Agenda

2030'). 'If tax dollars are used to bail out corporations, they must be utilized to promote green jobs and long-term, inclusive growth.' It should not save polluting, carbon-intensive businesses that are outmoded.'

This course of action will result in the unemployment of hundreds of thousands, if not millions, of people in Europe alone, as well as widespread poverty. To avoid a widespread rebellion, the empire is de facto expropriating and/or nationalizing various enterprises with government assistance, giving the empire complete control over the nature and future of these enterprises - if they are permitted to exist at all.

Both agendas have been signed by the European government, which has been following an active program for years to cause irreversible damage to European agriculture, economy, energy supply, and society in order to accomplish Agenda-2030, for which the EU's 'Green New Deal' was also developed.

Our other books

Check out our other books for other unreported news, exposed facts and debunked truths, and more.

Join the exclusive Rebel Press Media Circle!

You will get a new updates about the unreported reality delivered in your inbox every Friday.

Sign up here today:

https://campsite.bio/rebelpressmedia